My First Acrostic

The UK

Edited by Mark Richardson

First published in Great Britain in 2011 by:

Remus House
Coltsfoot Drive
Peterborough
PE2 9BF
Telephone: 01733 890066
Website: www.youngwriters.co.uk

All Rights Reserved
© Copyright Contributors 2011
SB ISBN 978-0-85739-461-3

Foreword

The 'My First Acrostic' collection was developed by Young Writers specifically for Key Stage 1 children. The poetic form is simple, fun and gives the young poet a guideline to shape their ideas, yet at the same time leaves room for their imagination and creativity to begin to blossom.

Due to the young age of the entrants we have enjoyed rewarding their effort by including as many of the poems as possible. Our hope is that seeing their work in print will encourage the children to continue writing as they grow and develop their skills into our poets of tomorrow.

Young Writers was established in 1990 to nurture creativity in our children and young adults, to give them an interest in poetry and an outlet to express themselves. This latest collection will act as a milestone for the young poets and one that will be enjoyable to revisit again and again.

Contents

All Saints' CW Primary School, Llanedeyrn
Jessica George (7) 1
Naomi Harries (7) 1
Kimberly Davies (7) 2
Jack Ataou (6) 2
Victoria Owen (7) 3

All Saints' RC Primary School, Glossop
Emmie Coffey (6) 3
William Jackson (7) 4
Jonathan Matthews (6) 5
Luke Ofori (7) 6
Clainey Marshall (6) 6
Shannon Jarratt (5) 7
Jacob Hanna (6) 7
Eleftheria Haley-Evdemon (5) 8
Joseph Done (6) 8
Niamh Johnson (5) 9

Billingborough Primary School, Billingborough
Ashleigh Watson (5) 9
Nicole Topham-Clark (5) 10
Chloe Inman (4) 11

Carlton Miniott CP School, Thirsk
Freddie Todd (5) 11
Matthew Brown (6) 12
Coby Tindall (5) 12
Emily Jackson (6) 13
Bethan Palfreeman (5) 13
Leila Roots (5) 14
Christopher Welford (6) 14
Saraya Johnson (5) 15
Milo Van Parys (6) 15
Alana Hamshaw-Stuart (6) 16
Amelia MacMillan (5) 16
Jack Zebedee (6) 17
Hollie Millward (5) 17
Josie Hargrave (5) 18
Katie Smith (5) 18
Macy Todd (6) 19

Ellie Mercer (6) 19
Caitlyn Large (5) 20

Dovedale Primary School, Nottingham
Jack Pearson (6) 20
Maddie Elliot (5) 21
Harvey Ryan (6) 21
Adam Aicha (6) 22
Georgia Ibberson (5) 22
Amber Shepherd (6) 23
Ellie Howe (5) 23
Liam Allsop (5) 24
Tia Proudlove (6) 24
Ellis Sanders (4) 25
Max Rowlinson (6) 25
Elizabeth Macfarlane (5) 26
Elissa Tyler (4) 26

Escrick CE Primary School, York
Joshua O'Connell (5) 27
Ryan Barry (5) 27
Gethin Blake (6) 28
Joseph Gibson (6) 28
Georgina Lewis (6) 29
Natasha O'Boyle (7) 29
William Cottingham (6) 30
Elliott Penn (6) 30
Sebastian Baden-Thomas (7) 31
Olivia Page (7) 31
Sam Askham (6) 32

Fairfield Primary School, Grimsby
Max Shipman (6) 32
Ruth Kersey (5) 33

Gosberton House School, Gosberton
Kyle Featherstone-Cole (6) 33
Bailey Johnson (6) 34
Dylan Chambers (6) 34

Hartsholme Primary School, Lincoln
Megan Hurst (6) 35
Devon Marshall (6) 35
Ben Asher (5) 36

Shay Purdy (5) 36
Thomas Clarke (6) 37
Jake Dunlop (5) 37
Elizabeth Rose (5) 38
Mia Harley-Beckett (6)...................... 38
Mollie Turner (6) 39

Kniveton CE Primary School, Kniveton

Alex Radlett (6) 39
Matthew Staniforth Armstrong (7)...... 40
Jasmine Heras (7)............................. 40
Jake Bayley (6) 41
Symi Chakma-Hawksworth (6) 41
Ethan Walsh (7)................................. 42
Lucie Crellin (6) 42

La Houguette Primary School, Guernsey

Amelia Hart (6) 43
Minnie Carré (7)................................ 43
Ruby Parker (6).................................. 44
Izabella Dupre (7).............................. 44
Samuel Bourgaize (7) 45
Jamie-Leigh Harvey (7) 45
Lola Johnson (7) 46
Amy Hill (6).. 46
Jack Bougourd (7)............................. 47
Pierre Pinchemain (7) 47
Oscar Oliver (6) 48
François Le Poidevin (6).................... 48
Olivia Edwards (6).............................. 49

Lakes CP School, Redcar

Isabelle Bailey & Grace (6)............... 49
Piper Clements & Kyle 50
Noah Sedgewick (7)......................... 50
Alex Dixon & Ellis 51
Callum Moore & Kalum 51
Paige & Katie Hunt (6) 52

Luddington & Garthorpe Primary School, Luddington

Jack Shaw (7).................................... 52
Sam Goodhand (6).......................... 53
Samantha Ratcliffe (7) 53
Charli-Brooke Lockwood (6)............. 54

Millfield Community Primary School, Heighington

Hannah Hemlin (6) 55
Adam Lockwood (6)......................... 55
Callum Thompson (6)....................... 56
Dylan White (6) 56
Jessica Smith (7)................................ 57
Finley Harrington Brown (6)............... 57
Laura Carter (6) 58

Mugginton CE Primary School, Ashbourne

Sophie Birks (6).................................. 58
Freya Leyland (5).............................. 59
Faye Meredith (6) 59
Emily Tatham (6)................................ 60

Myton Park Primary School, Stockton on Tees

Abigail Bone (5)................................ 60
Jacob Kelly 61
Joel West (7)..................................... 61
Emma Harvey (6) 62
Jacob Holmes (6).............................. 62
Erin Summersgill (5)........................... 63
Emillie Thomson (5)........................... 63
Nate Narroway (7) 64
Sophie Jones (6)................................ 64
Mia Nixon (6) 65
Ellie Nicholl (7) 65
Ellie McArdle (6)................................ 66
Lucy Dale (6) 66
Lucy Brown (6) 67
Tori Drummond (6)............................ 67
Alanna Garry-Madden (6)............... 68
Dylan Condren (7)............................ 68
Callum Wiedman (6)........................ 69
Jack Hughes (7) 69
Callum Reid (6) 70
Emma Watt (6).................................. 70

Thomas Latif (6) 71
Kacey Eyeington (5) 71
Chloe Ward (4) 72

Prenton Primary School, Prenton
George Farrell (7) 72
Emma Chapman (5) 73
James Roberts (5) 73
Emily Ellis (7)....................................... 74
Lucy Clayton (6) 74
Lily-Mae Hitchman (6)...................... 75
Ava Browne (4) 75
Hannah Martin (4) 76
Isabella Malam (5) 76
Alex Martin (7)..................................... 77
Emillia Young (5) 77
Charlie Oldfield (6) 78
Molly Richards-Carr (6) 78
Georgia Birch (5) 79
Amy Kendrick (6) 79
Sam Thomas (7) 80
Ellie Beecham (7) 80
Nyree Bennett (5).............................. 81
Yioula Ellina (7) 81
Benjamin Jones White (5) 82
Poppy Hunt (4)................................... 83
Jack Highe (7) 83
Olivia Williams (4)............................... 84
Callum Wynne (5).............................. 85
Lucy Williams (4) 86
Gemima Ellis (7) 87
Emilee Griffiths (7).............................. 88

Quadring Cowley & Brown's Primary School, Spalding
Harry Packard (5).............................. 89
Andreas Staggs (4) 89
Scott Askew (5) 90
Aimee Laud (4).................................. 90
Sophie Buchanan (4)....................... 91
Lois Boothby (5) 91
Joseph Hall (4)................................... 92
Kevin Burns (4) 92
Hayden Allen (4)................................ 93
Dimitris Staggs (6) 93
Ben Laud (6) 94
Hayley Reed (6)................................. 94

St Faith's CE Infant School, Lincoln
Sophie Tompkins (7).......................... 95
Catalina Collins (6) 95
Owen Hobden (6) 96
Elena Dent (6) 96
Jamie Brown (6) 97
Isobella Walker (7) 97
Archie Olivier-Townrow (7) 98
William Holden (6) 98
Isaac Atherton (7).............................. 99
Holli-May Davison (7) 99
Georgia Abbott (6) 100
Tommy Jameson (7) 100
Danielle Burrows (7) 101
Charlotte Drakard (6)...................... 101
Oliver Wiles (6) 102
Anna Gill (6)...................................... 102

St Patrick's RC Primary School, Walton-le-Dale
Jonathan Rigby (6)......................... 103
Alex Bateson (6)............................... 103
Lily Singleton (7) 104
Milly Thomas (6)............................... 104
Louana Avison (6)............................ 105
Grace Brown (6) 105
Sam Wilson (6).................................. 106
Faye Houghton (7) 106
Alexandra Fliegauf (6) 107
Tidus Nixon (6).................................. 107
Erin Rigby (7)..................................... 108
Matthew Simmons (7)...................... 108
Oliver Henderson (6)........................ 109
James Danby (6).............................. 109
Caitlin Ward (5)................................ 110
Taylor Howarth (6) 110
Olivia Grindley (5) 111
Leon Murphy (5) 111
Bradley Norwell (6).......................... 112

Samuel Barlow Primary School, Clipstone
Samuel Truscott (6).......................... 112
Blaize Smith (7) 113
Macy Bradley (6) 113
Aidan Riley (5) 114

Sowerby CP School, Thirsk

Sadie Askew (5) 114
Hope Smith (5) 115
Calum Kirby (5) 115
Francesca Kee (4) 116
Skye Beattie (4) 116
William Kelly (4) 117
Adam Cropper (5) 117
India Duree (4) 118
Bethan Ballard (4) 118
Riley Beighton (5) 119
Daniel Hindmarch (5) 119
Felicity Stockdale (4) 120
Sam Powell (4) 120
Eloise Christon (4) 121
RubyMai Cousins (5) 121
Taylor Clark (5) 122
Cameron Ord (4) 122
Kyle Pounder (5) 123

Stanwick Primary School, Wellingborough

Aaron Lovell (5) 123
Carla Hartley (5) 124
Evie McKay (4) 124
Grace Williams (5) 125
Jack Rhoder (4) 125
Maisy-Jay Wooding (4) 126
Megan Stuchfield (5) 126
Samuel Danton (4) 127
Scarlett King (5) 127
Sophie Lewis (4) 128
Taylor Lewis (5) 128
Yasmin Hussain (4) 129
Darcy Stanton (4) 129
Taylor Holben (5) 130
Owen Binks (6) 130
Harley Barker (5) 131
Skye Broomhead (6) 131
Rachel Hill (6) 132
Haylie Smith (6) 132
Eddie Phillips (6) 133
Michaela Dunn (6) 133
Lola Vukovic (5) 134
Caleb Neithercut (5) 134
Bethan Fraser (5) 135

Harris John (5) 135
Madeline Williams (5) 136
Tamzin Lineham (7) 136
Harrison Shouler (6) 137
Heidi Long (6) 137
Charlie Russell (7) 138
Ryan Smith (7) 138
Megan Breakwell (7) 139
Ciaran Baggott (7) 139
Callum Castle-Palmer (6) 140
Craig Dodson (7) 140
William Hobbs (6) 141
Toby Johnson (7) 141

Warwick Primary School, Wellingborough

Morgan Lewis (7) 142
Luke Hughes (7) 142
Bobby Ireland (6) 143
Robin Bayes (7) 143
Henry Lawley (7) 144
Kian Brown (6) 144
Jack Presley (6) 145
Chanelle McFarlane (6) 145
Rico Fensom (6) 146
Taylor Savage (6) 146
Corey Tyler (6) 147
Amber Davis (6) 147
Ellie Knighton (6) 148
Raajus Dewan (7) 148
Rebekah Shaw (7) 149
Logan Westrop (6) 149
Kia Abbott (7) 150
Shaun Rupere 150
Lucy Gregory 151
Sky Sharp (7) 151
Louise Sharp 152
Ella Louise Skeen (6) 152
Ellie Jones-King 153
Tia Warwick-Compton 153
Sava Trkulja 154
Chloe Bates 154
Charlie Rogers (6) 155
Cameron Daniels (7) 155
Ramzan Ali 156

Welbourn CE Primary School, Lincoln
Sean Appleton (6) 156
Darci Rose John (6) 157
Rachael Bain (6) 157
Patrick Mack (5) 158
Jack Livingstone (7) 158
Molly Holmes (7) 159
Lewis Stewart (5) 159
Tom Livingstone (5) 160
Chloe Francis (4) 160
Isabella Morris (4) 161
Teddy Tottingham (5) 161

The Poems

My First Acrostic 2011 - The UK

All About Jessica

J essica wants her name to be Jelly,
E njoys being strange,
S ometimes people think I'm
S illy.
I ndoors I watch fast moving TV.
C aterpillars are my favourite animal
A s they are skinny like me.

Jessica George (7)
All Saints' CW Primary School, Llanedeyrn

What Naomi Harries Likes

N aomi likes
A crositc poems about
O ctopuses
M aking blackish-bluey
I nk that is amazing for

H arrods' pens which are funny
A crostic poems are also good for describing
R ussell my exciting
R abbit so
I nteresting, huge hearted,
E xciting, loved
S o soft and cute and my favourite rabbit.

Naomi Harries (7)
All Saints' CW Primary School, Llanedeyrn

All About Fantastic Me

K imberly has super glasses.
I love
M y creative mummy. She is
B rilliant.
E llie is my super funny friend.
R oses are red and I love them.
L illies are white, they smell sweet.
Y outh club I go to on Friday.

Kimberly Davies (7)
All Saints' CW Primary School, Llanedeyrn

Jack

J umbo sausages
A re my favourite with a bottle of
C oke.
K ieren is my playful kitten

A nd he jumps a lot.
T rains are the best vehicle out of
A ll of them.
O btainers are my favourite part of the
U nique trains.

Jack Ataou (6)
All Saints' CW Primary School, Llanedeyrn

All About Super Me

V olcanoes are
I nteresting to me
C liffs are scary and make me
T errified
O cean sparkles when the sun shines on it
R ainbows show up when it is sunny and it rains
I like playing with my niece
A fter school.

Victoria Owen (7)
All Saints' CW Primary School, Llanedeyrn

Emmie Coffey

E mmie is always a star.
M agic in class, marvellous outside, sometimes very cheeky.
M oody Emmie sometimes really bossy.
I ntelligent me beating the class in maths.
E xcellent Emmie doing some good work.

C ool Emmie.
O utstanding Emmie in work.
F antastic crisp eater.
F un games that she makes up outside.
E xtremely good.
Y ummy things for dinner.

Emmie Coffey (6)
All Saints' RC Primary School, Glossop

William Jackson

Wonderful William
Incredible and super
Loves chocolate and
Loves ice creams
Interesting me
Amazing eater
Mr Clever Clogs

Just loves PS3s
Animals I like
Can't sing very well
Kind and sweet
Sleeps really well
Outstanding me
Nosy me.

William Jackson (7)
All Saints' RC Primary School, Glossop

My First Acrostic 2011 – The UK

Jonathan Matthews

J onathan is marvellous
O nly annoying sometimes
N osy Jonathan always
A mazing Jonathan at jumping
T he best in the class
H ighest marks in everything
A bsolutely amazing
N on-stop working

M aths I am good at
A mazing all the time
T errific boy
T he best boy
H elpful Jonathan
E xciting Jonathan
W as always looking for chocolate
S neaky boy.

Jonathan Matthews (6)
All Saints' RC Primary School, Glossop

Luke Ofori

L uke is a star.
U nbelievable me.
K ick-starting the day with a smile.
E xciting stories.

O range is not my favourite fruit.
F unny all day.
O utstanding work all day.
R unning all the time.
I nteresting boy.

Luke Ofori (7)
All Saints' RC Primary School, Glossop

Clainey Marshall

C lever clogs
L ove my puppet, Scampy
A crostic poem's just been written
I have yellow hair
N ice boy
E xciting
Y ummy yoghurt waiting to be eaten.

Clainey Marshall (6)
All Saints' RC Primary School, Glossop

My First Acrostic 2011 - The UK

Shannon Jarratt

S hannon is super-duper.

H elpful and a great friend.

A mazing girl.

N oodle Shannon.

N oisy girl Shannon.

O utstanding girl.

N ice girl Shannon is.

Shannon Jarratt (5)
All Saints' RC Primary School, Glossop

Jacob Hanna

J acob is nice.

A cting I like.

C aring and kind.

O n time.

B ouncy Jacob.

Jacob Hanna (6)
All Saints' RC Primary School, Glossop

Eleftheria Haley-Evdemon

E xcellent Eleftheria

L ovely Eleftheria

E legant Eleftheria

F antastic Eleftheria

T errific things

H ard work

E verything is special

R unner girl

I nteresting girl

A mazing Eleftheria.

Eleftheria Haley-Evdemon (5)
All Saints' RC Primary School, Glossop

Joseph Done

J ust be good, my grandma tells me.

O tters are good.

S uper at work.

E xciting boy.

P lays nicely.

H elpful.

D oes everything he's told.

O utstanding.

N ice and tall.

E ats fish and chips.

Joseph Done (6)
All Saints' RC Primary School, Glossop

My First Acrostic 2011 - The UK

Niamh Johnson

N ice Niamh all the time
I nteresting and exciting
A mazing and magic girl
M arvellous all the time
H elpful every day.

Niamh Johnson (5)
All Saints' RC Primary School, Glossop

Ashleigh

A pples are nice
S leep in my bed
H appy
L ove my family
E at honey on toast
I ce cream is yummy
G ran takes me to the shops
H elp Nicole tidy up

W riting is my favourite
A nd reading too
T eddy and Minnie are my toys
S inging is my favourite
O range juice is yummy
N icole is my friend.

Ashleigh Watson (5)
Billingborough Primary School, Billingborough

Nicole

N icole is my name
I ce cream is my favourite
C erys is my friend
O range juice is my best drink
L ove my mummy
E at my tea

T oday I am at school
O ctober is Mummy and Daddy's birthday
P laying is fun
H appy when I'm with Mrs McCormack
A pples are my best fruit
M oney is for buying things
-
C ooking at school is fun
L ollies are my best treat
A nd in my new bed is the best
R eading from the library
K angaroos jump high like me.

Nicole Topham-Clark (5)
Billingborough Primary School, Billingborough

My First Acrostic 2011 - The UK

Chloe

C hloe is happy
H as a sister called Brooke
L ikes oranges and apples
O n my bed I bounce
E very day I watch some TV

I read my books
N ever naughty at school
M ummy loves me
A pples are my favourite fruit
N oodles are yummy and tomatoes are too.

Chloe Inman (4)
Billingborough Primary School, Billingborough

Friends

F riends are very, very kind
R un fast
I 'm going to my friend's
E verybody was playing
N ice friend
D on't fight
S ee my friend.

Freddie Todd (5)
Carlton Miniott CP School, Thirsk

Never Be Mean

F unny friends
R un to the park
I played with my friends
E verybody played
N ever be mean
D on't forget
S tay friends.

Matthew Brown (6)
Carlton Miniott CP School, Thirsk

Friends

F riends are there for playing with
R unning down the street
I 'm having lots of fun
E veryone having lots of fun
N ow fun games
D isco with my friends
S uper games to play.

Coby Tindall (5)
Carlton Miniott CP School, Thirsk

Friends Are For...

F riends are for playing with
R unning along the street
I nteresting games
E xtremely fun games
N ice people
D ancing at discos
S inging together.

Emily Jackson (6)
Carlton Miniott CP School, Thirsk

Friends

F riends are funny
R osie is my friend
I am funny all the time
E ach friend has fun games
N ice friends play with me
D o not push people
S it down when it is circle time.

Bethan Palfreeman (5)
Carlton Miniott CP School, Thirsk

Fun Friends

F riends need to be forgiving

R unning down the street with my friend

I need to be there when my friend has fallen over

E ach friend needs to play with each other

N ice people need to be nice to other people

D on't disagree with other people

S ay nice things to other people.

Leila Roots (5)
Carlton Miniott CP School, Thirsk

Friends

F riends are funny

R unning down the street

I 'm running down the street

E xtremely fun games

N ice people

D on't push people

S haring is polite.

Christopher Welford (6)
Carlton Miniott CP School, Thirsk

My First Acrostic 2011 - The UK

Friends Are Kind

F riends are kind
R eally helpful
I am friendly
E verybody playing
N ice friends
D ancing with me
S ometimes in the park.

Saraya Johnson (5)
Carlton Miniott CP School, Thirsk

Be Friends With Each Other

F riends are there for playing
R unning down the street
I 'm having lots of fun
E veryone having fun
N ow fun, fun games
D isco with my friends
S leepover at my friend's house.

Milo Van Parys (6)
Carlton Miniott CP School, Thirsk

Friends

F riends are for playing with
R unning along the street
I 'm having fun
E xtremely fun games
N ice people have a little walk
D on't push people over
S ing together.

Alana Hamshaw-Stuart (6)
Carlton Miniott CP School, Thirsk

Friends

F riends are nice
R eally funny
I was dancing
E verybody danced
N ever naughty
D on't shout
S miling at me.

Amelia MacMillan (5)
Carlton Miniott CP School, Thirsk

Friends

F riends are kind
R un in the park
I can play
E verybody was happy
N ice friends
D ance at the park
S pecial presents.

Jack Zebedee (6)
Carlton Miniott CP School, Thirsk

Friends

F riends will be by your side
R unning down the street
I like to play with my friends
E veryone is for playing
N ice to others and kind
D ancing with my friends
S inging with my friends.

Hollie Millward (5)
Carlton Miniott CP School, Thirsk

The Poem Of Friends

F riends are kind to you
R osie is my friend
I like my friends
E veryone likes me
N ever push
D ancing at discos with my friends
S ome people are bad.

Josie Hargrave (5)
Carlton Miniott CP School, Thirsk

Friends

F riends are fun
R un in the playground
I am nice
E verybody is my friend
N ever fight
D on't be mean
S tay friends.

Katie Smith (5)
Carlton Miniott CP School, Thirsk

Friends Like To Play

F riends are for playing with
R un with my friends
I am a brilliant friend
E verybody is best friends
N ice friends are kind
D o be my friends
S pecial friends.

Macy Todd (6)
Carlton Miniott CP School, Thirsk

Funny Playground

F riends are friendly
R unning in the park
I love to sing with my friends
E xtremely fun games
N ow fun games
D isagreeing in the park
S illy games in the park.

Ellie Mercer (6)
Carlton Miniott CP School, Thirsk

Friends

F riends are for playing with
R unning down the street
I have fun when I run
E ach friend has fun
N ice people have a little walk
D isagree with other people
S ay sorry when you hurt other people.

Caitlyn Large (5)
Carlton Miniott CP School, Thirsk

My Name

J umping
A pples
C ars
K ite.

Jack Pearson (6)
Dovedale Primary School, Nottingham

My First Acrostic 2011 - The UK

My Name

M ouse
A pples
D ancing
D ogs
I ce cream
E lliot.

Maddie Elliot (5)
Dovedale Primary School, Nottingham

My Name

H air
A pples
R ain
V ets
E at
Y o-yos

R andom
Y ellow
A nts
N osy.

Harvey Ryan (6)
Dovedale Primary School, Nottingham

My Name

A dam
D ad
A corns
M um

A nts
I ce cream
C ornflakes
H ungry
A nimals.

Adam Aicha (6)
Dovedale Primary School, Nottingham

My Name

G uinea pig
E nd
O range
R unning
G iggly
I ce cream
A corns.

Georgia Ibberson (5)
Dovedale Primary School, Nottingham

My Name

A mber
M ummy
B rown
E mma
R abbits.

Amber Shepherd (6)
Dovedale Primary School, Nottingham

Animal Fun

E lephants have big ears
L ong trunks to drink with
E lephants eat leaves
P eople like to ride on elephants
H e can break trees down
A nd he sits on them
N aughty elephant
T wirling around.

Ellie Howe (5)
Dovedale Primary School, Nottingham

Animal Fun

M onkey lost his mum
O h no
N aughty monkey
K ing of the jungle
E veryone swinging in the trees
Y ellow bananas being eaten everywhere.

Liam Allsop (5)
Dovedale Primary School, Nottingham

Animal Fun

P arrot so colourful
A parrot copying you
R ound and round he flies
R ed feathers
O range beak
T en parrots in the trees.

Tia Proudlove (6)
Dovedale Primary School, Nottingham

Animal Fun

M onkey met an elephant

O range monkeys

N ice monkey

K ing monkey in the water

E verywhere, going places

Y apping everywhere in the jungle.

Ellis Sanders (4)
Dovedale Primary School, Nottingham

Animal Fun

T igers are very strong

I can't kill a tiger

G obbles up steak

E veryone runs away

R oars like an earthquake.

Max Rowlinson (6)
Dovedale Primary School, Nottingham

Animal Fun

E lephants are strong
L ong and fat
E ating everything
P addling in the water
H appy elephants
A ngry elephants
N aughty elephants
T en elephants
S illy elephants.

Elizabeth Macfarlane (5)
Dovedale Primary School, Nottingham

Animal Fun

G reat big legs
I see him in the jungle
R eally tall
A very long neck
F riendly giraffe
F unny giraffe
E verywhere.

Elissa Tyler (4)
Dovedale Primary School, Nottingham

My First Acrostic 2011 – The UK

My Name Is Josh!

J olly Joshua

O n the

S lide

H aving fun.

Joshua O'Connell (5)
Escrick CE Primary School, York

My Name

R ushing Ryan loves

Y oghurt for breakfast

A nd dinner

N icks some of Dylan's yoghurt.

Ryan Barry (5)
Escrick CE Primary School, York

All About Gethin

G reat Gethin

E ats ham and

T omatoes

H appy

I nside

N ever sad.

Gethin Blake (6)
Escrick CE Primary School, York

Joseph's Bike Ride

J olly Joseph

O n the bike

S peeding fast

E xercising

P eddling past

H annah.

Joseph Gibson (6)
Escrick CE Primary School, York

A Cat Toy

C uddly, so cute

A s can be

T oday I love you and my daddy.

Georgina Lewis (6)
Escrick CE Primary School, York

My Teddy

T oday my teddy lost his head and

E veryone looked under the bed

D id they find it?

D id they hide him?

Y es they did.

Natasha O'Boyle (7)
Escrick CE Primary School, York

What William Likes

W obbly Will likes tomatoes and ice cream and

I cky cream and

L icky lollies and

L emonade.

William Cottingham (6)
Escrick CE Primary School, York

My Teddy

T iny teddy bear come to me.

E ven I have a teddy bear.

D o you need a friend?

D o you want to stay with me?

Y es I do!

Elliott Penn (6)
Escrick CE Primary School, York

My First Acrostic 2011 - The UK

What I Think Of Lego

L ego is really fun
E veryone likes Lego
G reatest Lego ever I think is Prince of Persia
O n the table is where we build it.

Sebastian Baden-Thomas (7)
Escrick CE Primary School, York

Dolls

D ifferent dolls all over the world
O ne is white and one is brown
L ots of lovely things they do
L augh and cry
S ing and shout.

Olivia Page (7)
Escrick CE Primary School, York

My Teddy Bear

T eddy, teddy, where are you?
E veryone looked in the zoo
D id they find him
D own the loo?
Y es, it's true.

Sam Askham (6)
Escrick CE Primary School, York

The Army

A rmy on parade showing their swords and uniforms
R un in the mud
M ajor and corporal like parachuting
Y ahoo shout the army, work had finished!

Max Shipman (6)
Fairfield Primary School, Grimsby

My First Acrostic 2011 - The UK

All About Me

R uth likes food
U p to mischief
T eeth are pretty
H as blonde hair.

Ruth Kersey (5)
Fairfield Primary School, Grimsby

My Favourite Toy

S uper
P ink
I nteresting
N ice
N ice
E xciting
R ed.

Kyle Featherstone-Cole (6)
Gosberton House School, Gosberton

My Favourite Toy

T homas
R ailway
A lbert
I sland of Sodor
N eville.

Bailey Johnson (6)
Gosberton House School, Gosberton

My Favourite Toy

C ome
A nd
R ace
S nakes.

Dylan Chambers (6)
Gosberton House School, Gosberton

Jester

J uggling jester
E xciting
S carlet twisty shoes
T umbling, twirling
E ntertaining
R unning, entertaining.

Megan Hurst (6)
Hartsholme Primary School, Lincoln

Jester

J olly jokes
E xcited king and queen
S illy jester
T iptoe happily
E nergetic, dancing
R ed, purple, green spots.

Devon Marshall (6)
Hartsholme Primary School, Lincoln

Jester

J umping
E xcited
S illy
T umbling
E nergetic
R unning.

Ben Asher (5)
Hartsholme Primary School, Lincoln

Jester

J umping
E xciting
S illy
T ickling
E nergetic
R unning.

Shay Purdy (5)
Hartsholme Primary School, Lincoln

My First Acrostic 2011 - The UK

Jester

J okes are funny
E nergetic and funny
S illy scarlet shoes
T iptoeing and travelling
E xcited king and queen
R unning, running in his red shoes.

Thomas Clarke (6)
Hartsholme Primary School, Lincoln

Silly Jester

J uggling and juggling and jokes
E nergetic jumping
S carlet and yellow costume
T iptoes on his toes
E xcellent jester
R olling on the table.

Jake Dunlop (5)
Hartsholme Primary School, Lincoln

Jester

J ingle bells jingle
E xciting the king and queen
S illy dancing
T wirls around
E ntertain the king and queen
R unning fast, super fast.

Elizabeth Rose (5)
Hartsholme Primary School, Lincoln

Jumping Jester

J olly jumping
E ntertaining king and queen
S illy shoes
T umbling in the castle
E xcited jester
R ed and yellow hat.

Mia Harley-Beckett (6)
Hartsholme Primary School, Lincoln

Jolly Jester

J uggling balls

E xciting jester

S hiny jester

T iptoeing

E nergetic

R ed hat.

Mollie Turner (6)
Hartsholme Primary School, Lincoln

Cassowary

C atch it if you can

A lways making a noise

S tamps its feet

S ort of strange

O n the ground

W alking bird

A nest made of leaves

R are to find

Y ou must be gentle with it.

Alex Radlett (6)
Kniveton CE Primary School, Kniveton

Magpie

M ischievous magpies
A llowed to roam free
G liding above our heads
P erching in the trees
I n the sky I see them fly
E ating anything they can find.

Matthew Staniforth Armstrong (7)
Kniveton CE Primary School, Kniveton

Eagle

E xciting
A nnoying to others
G obbling
L ifting
E legant.

Jasmine Heras (7)
Kniveton CE Primary School, Kniveton

My First Acrostic 2011 - The UK

Swan

S wimming swan
W avy lake
A beautiful bird
N ice swan.

Jake Bayley (6)
Kniveton CE Primary School, Kniveton

Robin

R ed breast
O pening its little beak
B eautiful bird
I n its warm, snug and cosy
N est.

Symi Chakma-Hawksworth (6)
Kniveton CE Primary School, Kniveton

Magpie

M eddling
A nnoying
G liding
P est
I n the sky I see
E ating.

Ethan Walsh (7)
Kniveton CE Primary School, Kniveton

Penguin

P layful
E ating
N aughty
G lancing
U nder the water
I n a pool
N ice.

Lucie Crellin (6)
Kniveton CE Primary School, Kniveton

Spring

S unny days.

P urple flowers.

R oses bloom red and pink.

I ce is gone, sun is up.

N ice ripe food, fresh from the tree.

G reen trees are really fun.

Amelia Hart (6)
La Houguette Primary School, Guernsey

Sunny Time

S o light, like yellow.

U nbelievable.

N ever like the night sky.

N ew to everyone who's just been born.

Y ay, the sun has come out.

T iptoeing when the sun goes down.

I n the sunlight, lots of light.

M aking us smile.

E nding lovely.

Minnie Carré (7)
La Houguette Primary School, Guernsey

Butterfly

B utterfly, you have lovely wings.

U sually flying.

T he best creature.

T he best flier.

E very day looking beautiful.

R ubbish at running but a good friend.

F lying gracefully.

L ovely butterfly.

Y ou must be popular.

Ruby Parker (6)
La Houguette Primary School, Guernsey

Gazelle

G azelle went over the hill and was leaping about in the hills.

A kite was flying in the air and the gazelle was trying to get it.

Z ebra was watching a gazelle running away from a hippo.

E lly the peacock was shouting, 'The race is about to begin.'

L iz the gazelle was going to have a baby and she was excited.

L ouisa the giraffe was excited because her friend was getting a trophy.

E lmin was shouting, 'Hip hip hooray.'

Izabella Dupre (7)
La Houguette Primary School, Guernsey

My First Acrostic 2011 – The UK

Football

F eet clambering about.
O nto the pitch they fly.
O h my gosh!
T eams running around.
B eing pushed and shoved.
A lready a penalty.
L earning how to get a score.
L iving with the winning goal.

Samuel Bourgaize (7)
La Houguette Primary School, Guernsey

Cat

C ats are nice and fluffy.
A re cute and naughty.
T hey are very cuddly.

Jamie-Leigh Harvey (7)
La Houguette Primary School, Guernsey

Teacher

T eaching my class, my teacher sits
E ven a bit of rain doesn't stop him
A lot of work today
C oming out to play in the playground with a friend
H earing the bell he let us out
E ating our snack from our lunchtime pack
R iding in the car on the way home.

Lola Johnson (7)
La Houguette Primary School, Guernsey

Dog

D inner time doggy
O utside time doggy for a walk
G oing home now doggy.

Amy Hill (6)
La Houguette Primary School, Guernsey

Dad And Me

D angerous
A dventurous
D ipping

A motorbike in the greenhouse
N ever moaning
D iving

M agical
E nd.

Jack Bougourd (7)
La Houguette Primary School, Guernsey

Red

R ed is the colour of Sylvans football club every Saturday
E xcited for Sylvans every Saturday
D ad, I'll have my red cup.

Pierre Pinchemain (7)
La Houguette Primary School, Guernsey

Goats

G etting grass to eat
O ver the hills, climbing up mountains
A lways running all around
T rying to headbutt anything in its way!

Oscar Oliver (6)
La Houguette Primary School, Guernsey

Hamster

H appy every day at night
A wesome, better than cute
M aize he loves to eat
S noring all day
T errified in the light
E very night awake
R esting all day.

François Le Poidevin (6)
La Houguette Primary School, Guernsey

Colours

C olourful colours.

O ver the hills there was a golf car which was green.

L ying on the yellow sand.

O pen the blue door.

U nder the blue sky

R ound and round went the golden sand.

S plash went the blue sea.

Olivia Edwards (6)
La Houguette Primary School, Guernsey

Horse

H unting all day

O r

R acing about

S leeping

E ating grass all day long.

Isabelle Bailey & Grace (6)
Lakes CP School, Redcar

Puppies

P uppies playing
U nder the table
P ushing
P awing
I nside their beds
E ating and
S leeping.

Piper Clements & Kyle
Lakes CP School, Redcar

Animal

A nteater
N ewt
I nsect
M onkey
A nt
L eopard.

Noah Sedgewick (7)
Lakes CP School, Redcar

My First Acrostic 2011 - The UK

Animal

A lex the lion of Madagascar
N ight eaters
I ncredible animals
M onkey
A nd
L eopard.

Alex Dixon & Ellis
Lakes CP School, Redcar

Fish

F ish swim in water
I nside wrecks
S plashing everywhere
H e swims fast.

Callum Moore & Kalum
Lakes CP School, Redcar

Puppy

P uppies are fun

U nhappy puppies

P uppies are cute

P uppies are hungry

Y ou can teach your puppies tricks.

Paige & Katie Hunt (6)
Lakes CP School, Redcar

Jack Shaw

J umping high

A nd good at building Lego

C an run fast

K icking a ball

S howing off

H arry is my friend

A lways a good boy

W ork hard.

Jack Shaw (7)
Luddington & Garthorpe Primary School, Luddington

Sam

S am's house is strong

A lways playing

M y house has a garden.

Sam Goodhand (6)
Luddington & Garthorpe Primary School, Luddington

Samantha

S amantha is my first name, Ratcliffe is my last

A nd I am seven years old

M ost of the time I am happy

A nd my favourite food is bacon sandwiches

N ow I only have my favourite food on Fridays

T he year I was born was 2004

H am sandwiches are really yummy

A nd my favourite teacher is Miss Rhodes.

Samantha Ratcliffe (7)
Luddington & Garthorpe Primary School, Luddington

Charli-Brooke

C heeky Charli-Brooke
H appy Charli-Brooke
A ge is six
R un with my friends
L ove my mummy
I love guinea pigs

B ake with my mummy
R eady for school
O range I love
O ver to my friend's house
K ind to my dog
E at all of my food.

Charli-Brooke Lockwood (6)
Luddington & Garthorpe Primary School, Luddington

My First Acrostic 2011 - The UK

Hannah Hemlin

H as pretty, long, blonde hair
A lways adventurous
N ever noisy
N ever nervous
A mazing me
H as pretty, long dresses and clothes.

Hannah Hemlin (6)
Millfield Community Primary School, Heighington

Adam Lockwood

A lways asking questions
D reaming about football
A nd never stops
M oaning.

Adam Lockwood (6)
Millfield Community Primary School, Heighington

Callum

C uddly
A pple eating
L ovely and juicy
L ovely and yummy
U p high in the tree
M uddy on the ground.

Callum Thompson (6)
Millfield Community Primary School, Heighington

About Dylan

D rawing super-duper pictures
Y ippee! I like to shout
L oves licking lovely lollipops
A fantastic footballer
N ever noisy in the library

W as quiet
H ates most purply-pink things
I love lots of sports
T ells Dad about school
E very day plays fun football.

Dylan White (6)
Millfield Community Primary School, Heighington

My First Acrostic 2011 - The UK

Jessica

J umping, having fun in the playground

E ating an apple

S itting on a chair

S eeing all the birds flying

I nside the paddling pool

C leaning myself

A nd having lots of fun.

Jessica Smith (7)
Millfield Community Primary School, Heighington

About Finley

F ootball mad

I ncredible at football

N oisy

L oud

E xcellent

Y ellow football shirt.

Finley Harrington Brown (6)
Millfield Community Primary School, Heighington

Laura

L ambs
A nimals
U mbrella
R apunzel
A mazing.

Laura Carter (6)
Millfield Community Primary School, Heighington

Sophie

S wimming is fun
O r running
P ainting outside
H elping my mum tidy up
I n the sun singing
E yes are beautiful.

Sophie Birks (6)
Mugginton CE Primary School, Ashbourne

My First Acrostic 2011 – The UK

Freya

F or my tea I like fish fingers

R eading is fun

E ats sandwiches

Y ou can't do what I can

A ll I like to do is play.

Freya Leyland (5)
Mugginton CE Primary School, Ashbourne

Faye

F or breakfast I like to have Branflakes with milk

A ll I like doing is swimming

Y ou know I like chips

E xercise is fun.

Faye Meredith (6)
Mugginton CE Primary School, Ashbourne

Emily

E njoy reading

M y favourite book

I n summer I

L ike playing in the paddling pool

Y ou know I like playing.

Emily Tatham (6)
Mugginton CE Primary School, Ashbourne

Playtime

P laytime is fun.

L ook, there's a new shed.

A ll the children play outside.

Y ou can play with me.

T remendous toys to play with.

I play with my friends.

M ore playtime!

E xciting playtime.

Abigail Bone (5)
Myton Park Primary School, Stockton on Tees

My First Acrostic 2011 - The UK

Playtime

'P laytime has come,' the children shout.
L ook, there's the second goal!
A pples get eaten with a munch.
Y es, let's play tig.
T oys get played with.
I think the bell is going to ring now.
M y friend always plays with me.
E veryone comes marching in a line.

Jacob Kelly
Myton Park Primary School, Stockton on Tees

Lion

L ong, thin nails.
I like to hunt day and night.
O n Saturday is my day for hunting.
N ever do I eat my babies, but I do eat human beings.

Joel West (7)
Myton Park Primary School, Stockton on Tees

Toys And Games

Toys to play with my friends!

Oh no, a toy broke.

You can come and play with me!

She is my best friend.

All the children play together.

No one wants to play with me.

Doors open at playtime.

Games are fun at playtime.

After playtime the bell rings!

Me and my friend go to the friendship stop.

Everyone plays at playtime.

She said, 'Are you my friend?'

Emma Harvey (6)
Myton Park Primary School, Stockton on Tees

Bear

Black and soft

Everyone hunts me

A creature with big paws

Rotten teeth.

Jacob Holmes (6)
Myton Park Primary School, Stockton on Tees

Playtime

P lay in the playground

L ots of my friends play with me

A ll of us play together nicely

Y es, it's playtime

T hey are running fast

I like the playground

M ake friends

E ach person is running past me.

Erin Summersgill (5)
Myton Park Primary School, Stockton on Tees

Playground

P laying in the playground

L ittle friends playing

A ll the friends giggling

Y ellow sunny sun

G reen grass growing

R ocking chairs rocking

O n the hill we run

U nder the tree we're chatting

N oisy people playing

D o you want to play with me?

Emillie Thomson (5)
Myton Park Primary School, Stockton on Tees

Cat

C laws and teeth are both sharp
A t all times I'm alert to people
T ail up all day long and night.

Nate Narroway (7)
Myton Park Primary School, Stockton on Tees

Tiger

T eeth are sharp and pointy
I have golden eyes
G ood creatures
E ach animal I see with my golden eyes I will eat for breakfast
R ushing in the green grass.

Sophie Jones (6)
Myton Park Primary School, Stockton on Tees

My First Acrostic 2011 - The UK

Rabbit

R uffly body
A very cuddly and furry ball
B ouncy animal
B een to other homes before
I t eats day and night
T ons and tons of food.

Mia Nixon (6)
Myton Park Primary School, Stockton on Tees

Lion

L ong teeth are sharp
I am fierce
O n the ground I pound
N ight comes and I hunt for animals. I eat them.

Ellie Nicholl (7)
Myton Park Primary School, Stockton on Tees

Bunny

B ouncing all day long

U p and down every day racing myself

N ow, when I'm going to get fed by my owner

N ever sleep at night

Y ou put me in a hutch.

Ellie McArdle (6)
Myton Park Primary School, Stockton on Tees

Cats

C uddles up on

A lap

T o keep

S nuggly warm.

Lucy Dale (6)
Myton Park Primary School, Stockton on Tees

Horse

H ooves on the road go clip-clop
O ver one metre high
R acing round the track is so much fun
S ometimes you might fall off me
E ating carrots is so yummy.

Lucy Brown (6)
Myton Park Primary School, Stockton on Tees

Bat

B lack wings flying at night
A bat eats fruit
T he teeth are long and dangerous.

Tori Drummond (6)
Myton Park Primary School, Stockton on Tees

Rabbit

R un as quick as a flash
A lazy thing
B lack and white
B ouncy thing
I t is soft
T ail is bouncing up and down.

Alanna Garry-Madden (6)
Myton Park Primary School, Stockton on Tees

Dog

D ancing and funny
O nce tea is ready they jump up on the table
G o for a walk and they will find a bone.

Dylan Condren (7)
Myton Park Primary School, Stockton on Tees

My First Acrostic 2011 – The UK

Lion

L ong, dangerous teeth.
I like to eat meat.
O n Sunday is the day that I go hunting.
N ight comes and I go out to hunt.

Callum Wiedman (6)
Myton Park Primary School, Stockton on Tees

Bat

B ats are black.
A re very fast when they fly and flap their wings.
T hey eat insects.

Jack Hughes (7)
Myton Park Primary School, Stockton on Tees

Lion

L ions are fierce and bad
I am dangerous and scary
O n my skin are patterns
N obody can scare a lion.

Callum Reid (6)
Myton Park Primary School, Stockton on Tees

Kitten

K eep me inside in stormy weather
I am really furry and cute like a dog
T ickly as ever when I'm tickled with a feather
T rouble when my eyes are open but leave me alone and I'll be good
E ating fish every day and night
N obody knows I'm out of sight.

Emma Watt (6)
Myton Park Primary School, Stockton on Tees

My First Acrostic 2011 - The UK

Tiger

T eeth are sharp and gorgeous

I like to purr

G ood cutters

E ach animal I see I eat

R ushing through the grass.

Thomas Latif (6)
Myton Park Primary School, Stockton on Tees

Humpty

H umpty cried on the wall

U p from the wall he fell

M um shouted at him

P oor Humpty

T o the egg hospital

Y ou are nearly better.

Kacey Eyeington (5)
Myton Park Primary School, Stockton on Tees

Humpty

H umpty fell off the wall
U p he climbed
M um was looking for him
P lease can you help him?
T he king's horses and the king's men couldn't mend Humpty
Y um-yum in my tum.

Chloe Ward (4)
Myton Park Primary School, Stockton on Tees

Transformers – More Than Meets The Eye

T ransform into anything
R obots in disguise
A utobots are the good guys
N obody knows where they are
S ideswipe is a warrior for the Autobots
F ast
O ptimus Prime is the leader of the Autobots
R otating gears in their joints
M egatron is the leader of the evil Decepticons
E ach one has different microchips
R atchet repairs battle damage
S aving the Earth is their job.

George Farrell (7)
Prenton Primary School, Prenton

My First Acrostic 2011 - The UK

Emma Is My Name

E mma is my name
M ary is my middle name
M y favourite colour is peach
A nd I like to play with Simon and Mummy

C hicken dinner is my favourite tea at Daddy's
H annah and Emma are my best friends
A pples are yummy in my lunchbox
P rincess Jasmine is my favourite doll
M ost days I like to dress up
A nimals are my favourite subject at school
N anny and Grandad are my special family.

Emma Chapman (5)
Prenton Primary School, Prenton

Star Wars

S paceships looking for General Grievous
T he Jedis lightsabers are bright
A fter Darth Vader and Darth Maul
R eady for a fight

W ill Obi Wan and Yoda win?
A re they going to save the day?
R eady to beat the darkside
S aving the galaxy far away.

James Roberts (5)
Prenton Primary School, Prenton

My First Poem

E mily is a twin
M y sister is called Gemima
I like having fun
L aughing and jumping
Y es and always beside her

E ats lots of fruit
L ikes healthy food
L ikes school
I even like my teacher
S o everything is cool.

Emily Ellis (7)
Prenton Primary School, Prenton

Lucy Clayton's List Of Favourite Things

L ucy's list of favourite things
U mm, chocolate bars make me sing
C ooking with Mum is really fun
Y esterday she made a bun

C omputer games are really cool
L ove to read when I am in school
A nother thing just fine for me
Y es, I love to watch TV
T o drink warm milk, don't spill, make a mess
O h, nearly forgot my Nintendo DS
N othing makes me happier than playing with my baby brother, William.

Lucy Clayton (6)
Prenton Primary School, Prenton

My First Acrostic 2011 - The UK

Lily-Mae Hitchman

L ily-Mae, I'm nearly 6
I n the morning for breakfast I have Weetabix
L ove to sing, dance and play
Y es, I could sing and dance all day
-
M egan is my friend in school
A nd we like to go to the swimming pool
E ating sweets and having fun

H elping tidy up with Mum
I n school I work and play with friends
T hen get strawberry ice cream when it ends
C allum, my brother, likes mint choc chip
H ere's my sister, Sophie, with a chocolate dip
M y favourite colour in the world is pink
A ll my friends like it too
N ot the boys though, they like blue!

Lily-Mae Hitchman (6)
Prenton Primary School, Prenton

Ava Browne

A va Browne is 4
V ery soon she is 5
A ll she does is play.

Ava Browne (4)
Prenton Primary School, Prenton

Hannah Martin

Hannah is a superhero

Alex is the best big sister

Nanna is nice

Never go near a fire

Aunty Kate is my mate

Hurricane Hannah gets a strike

My favourite food is fish and chips

All the fairies are the best

Richard is my daddy

'Toy Story 2 makes me happy

I love all my family

Nicest ice cream is mint choc chip.

Hannah Martin (4)
Prenton Primary School, Prenton

Barbie Girl

I like Lotso the bear

See that unicorn over there, it is beautiful

Always kind to my friends

Bella means beautiful in Italian

Emma is my mummy's name

Lovely Mary is my best friend

Lakes have lots of fish

Amen is said at the end of a prayer in church.

Isabella Malam (5)
Prenton Primary School, Prenton

My First Acrostic 2011 - The UK

Alex Martin

A ngel Alex is 7
L ovely Louise is my mum
E llie is my best friend
X -Factor is great

M adeline is my favourite programme
A pepperoni pizza is perfect
R icky Sting is my dad's bowling name
T hursday is my swimming day
I believe in God
N othing stops Alex.

Alex Martin (7)
Prenton Primary School, Prenton

Eating Strawberries

E ating strawberries
M akes me smile
I 'm eating strawberries all the while
L ovely, juicy and oh so squishy
L ots and lots of them in my dishy
I love strawberries in a great big pile
A nd that's what always makes me smile

Y ummy, yummy
O h so scrummy
U nderneath my ice cream they hide
N ever ever leave too many, oh
G orgeous strawberries by my side.

Emillia Young (5)
Prenton Primary School, Prenton

Christmas

C hristmas is here
H ear the bells ring
R udolph is flying
I t's Christmas
S anta is coming
T insel wrapped around the tree
M ake sure you are good
A sk your parents to leave food
S anta is stuck down the chimney.

Charlie Oldfield (6)
Prenton Primary School, Prenton

Skipping

M olly can skip
O ver the rope
L oving to skip fast
L aughing with a smile
Y ou can skip too.

Molly Richards-Carr (6)
Prenton Primary School, Prenton

Royden Park

R obins tweeting

O utdoor beauty

Y oungsters playing

D ucks quacking and

E ating our bread

N ature

P eaceful walks

A ll aboard the

R ailway train

K ids having fun.

Georgia Birch (5)
Prenton Primary School, Prenton

Rainbow

R ed is the first colour in the rainbow

A n arch is in the sky

I can see indigo way up high

N o one can find the gold

B lue is the fifth colour

O range is nice and bright

W atching through my window when it is light.

Amy Kendrick (6)
Prenton Primary School, Prenton

Family

F un is my family

A ll you ever need is a family

M y brother Ben

I love my family

L ucky you have a family

Y ou would be lonely without a family.

Sam Thomas (7)
Prenton Primary School, Prenton

A Lovely Day

E very day

L ittle May

L oved to play

I n the park

E ven though the doggies bark.

Ellie Beecham (7)
Prenton Primary School, Prenton

My First Acrostic 2011 - The UK

Disco

D ancing to the music
I n my disco class
S inging to my teacher
C Ds playing loud
O h what fun it is!

Nyree Bennett (5)
Prenton Primary School, Prenton

Yioula Ellina

Y oghurt is my favourite snack
I love the colour pink
O ne day I want to be a pop star
U p on stage is where I dance
L ollipops are my favourite sweet
A holiday in Greece

E lizabeth is my best friend
L ucy is my dog's name
L ooking at the stars is amazing
I have an older sister
N orthwood Road is where I live
A lexandra is my sister's name.

Yioula Ellina (7)
Prenton Primary School, Prenton

Football

B all is dribbled towards the goal
E veryone cheers with all their soul
N o one can catch me, I'm too fast
J umping and dodging those I run past
A pproaching the goal, I see it in sight
M any try to catch me with all their might
I 'm ready to shoot as I hear the crowd
N othing can stop me as the cheers grow loud

J oy on my mum and dad's faces as they watch me
O nwards I go, how proud they will be
N ow is the time. I lift back my leg
E veryone gasps and begins to beg
S houting now stops as all hold their breath

W ill time run out, they all look to the ref
H olding out his hands, the goalie gets into position
I 've kicked the ball hard, it's now on a mission
T he goalie dives right, to the ball he will get
E veryone goes wild, back of the net.

Benjamin Jones White (5)
Prenton Primary School, Prenton

My First Acrostic 2011 - The UK

Beautiful

B utterflies have beautiful wings
E very time I see them
A ll different colours
U p and down
T hey go
I t makes me happy
F lap your wings
U p and down
L ovely butterflies.

Poppy Hunt (4)
Prenton Primary School, Prenton

Snuggle

S ometimes I like to snuggle
N ext to my mummy
U p in my room
G oing to bed with my teddy
G etting comfy and sleepy
L istening to my mummy's story
E very day I love to snuggle.

Jack Highe (7)
Prenton Primary School, Prenton

Me

Olivia is 4 years old
Lives at home with Mummy
I like sweeties very much
Very confident I am
Interested in dancing
And I sing very loud

Watching CBeebies is fun
I have a cat called Magic
Listening to music makes me happy
Learning to ride a bike
I support Everton like Daddy
All I do is giggle
My favourite colour is pink
Swimming is my hobby.

Olivia Williams (4)
Prenton Primary School, Prenton

Callum Cheestring

C all me Callum Cheestring
A ll day long I eat cheese
L ike cheese
L ove cheese
U pset without cheese
M ore cheese please!

W hy do I like cheese?
Y ummy yummy in my tummy
N ot allowed too much cheese
N ot fair, Mum please!
E ach and every day - cheese! Cheese! Cheese!

Callum Wynne (5)
Prenton Primary School, Prenton

Lucy Williams

L ucy is my name
U nder the duvet I love to snuggle
C uddles I give lots of
Y ou couldn't ask for more

W hen I play with Barbie
  I dress her in pink clothes
  L ots of lovely laughing
  L ots of loud noise
  I like to play with Grandma and Grandad
A nd my school friends
M ummy, Daddy and my family love me loads
  S o I'm a happy girl.

Lucy Williams (4)
Prenton Primary School, Prenton

My First Poem

G emima is my name
E lephants make me run
M y favourite dance is ballet, it's true
I like having fun
M y mummy is the best
A lways trust her I know she is the best

E ating chips I enjoy
L oving animals
L oving Sam's guinea pigs
I ts cute face
S o soft and furry too.

Gemima Ellis (7)
Prenton Primary School, Prenton

My Name

E milee likes chocolate

M um is kind

I n our house we have 7 people

L aughing is fun in our house

E very morning I have breakfast

E very night I have tea

G rizzly Tales for Gruesome Kids is my favourite show

R ed is my favourite colour

I like muffins

F riends make me happy

F rogs eat flies

I like weekends

T here are times when me and Dave go to the shop

H arry Potter is my favourite film as well

S ausage butties are yummy.

Emilee Griffiths (7)
Prenton Primary School, Prenton

Fairy Tale Characters

C leaned the house

I nvitation to the party

N ice Fairy Godmother

D anced with the prince

E xcited to be at the party

R ags for clothes

E njoyed herself at the party

L onely

L eft her glass slipper

A nd they all lived happily ever after.

Harry Packard (5)
Quadring Cowley & Brown's Primary School, Spalding

Fairy Tale Characters

J ack sold his cow

A nd got some magic beans

C limbs the beanstalk

K eeps the gold.

Andreas Staggs (4)
Quadring Cowley & Brown's Primary School, Spalding

Fairy Tale Characters

J olly
A poor boy
C limbed the beanstalk
K nelt under the table.

Scott Askew (5)
Quadring Cowley & Brown's Primary School, Spalding

Fairy Tale Characters

G reedy
O pened the door
L ong golden hair
D ecided to try the porridge
I n the bears' house
L ost in the woods
O nly liked Baby Bear's things
C hose Baby Bear's chair
K nocked once on the door
S lept in Baby Bear's bed.

Aimee Laud (4)
Quadring Cowley & Brown's Primary School, Spalding

Fairy Tale Characters

G reedy
I n the sky
A ngry
N asty
T errible voice.

Sophie Buchanan (4)
Quadring Cowley & Brown's Primary School, Spalding

Fairy Tale Characters

B aby bed
A boy bear
B aby bowl
Y oung

B roken chair
E mpty bowl
A ngry
R an after Goldilocks.

Lois Boothby (5)
Quadring Cowley & Brown's Primary School, Spalding

Fairy Tale Characters

Golden hair

Opened the door

Liked porridge

Didn't ask

Invited herself in

Lost in the woods

Only Baby Bear's was just right

Called inside

Knocked on the door

Sat in their chairs.

Joseph Hall (4)
Quadring Cowley & Brown's Primary School, Spalding

Fairy Tale Characters

Gobbles up the porridge

Only likes Baby Bear's chair

Lets herself in the house

Doesn't like Daddy Bear's chair

In the woods

Long yellow hair

Only likes Baby Bear's porridge

Cracks Baby Bear's chair

Knocks but nobody answers

Sleeps in Baby Bear's bed.

Kevin Burns (4)
Quadring Cowley & Brown's Primary School, Spalding

Fairy Tale Characters

T oo big for Mummy's house
H ouse of straw
R eally nasty wolf
E ach pig builds a house
E aten by the wolf

P ot of boiling water
I n the fire
G oes down the chimney
S trong brick house.

Hayden Allen (4)
Quadring Cowley & Brown's Primary School, Spalding

Me, Myself And I

D angerous
I s a fast runner
M imee is my nickname
I s happy
T idy
R eady
I n Woodpecker's class he
S ings.

Dimitris Staggs (6)
Quadring Cowley & Brown's Primary School, Spalding

Me, Myself And I

B oy who is
E xciting and
N ice

L ovely
A mbitious
U mbrella
D inosaur.

Ben Laud (6)
Quadring Cowley & Brown's Primary School, Spalding

Me, Myself And I

H elping Hayley
A lways helping
Y ounger children
L ikes turtles and
E verything about her is good
Y oung dancer

R eady to help
E verybody
E ven
D ogs.

Hayley Reed (6)
Quadring Cowley & Brown's Primary School, Spalding

Earth

E arth is my home
A ll animals are different
R eally this is my home
T he Earth is my place
H ome makes me safe.

Sophie Tompkins (7)
St Faith's CE Infant School, Lincoln

The Sun

S un sizzling
U p in the sky
N ever look at the sun.

Catalina Collins (6)
St Faith's CE Infant School, Lincoln

The Sun

S teaming sun

U p in the blue sky

N ever touch the sun.

Owen Hobden (6)
St Faith's CE Infant School, Lincoln

Earth

E arth is elegant

A mazing Earth

R efreshing food and water

T he world is amazing

H ome to me.

Elena Dent (6)
St Faith's CE Infant School, Lincoln

Earth

E very animal is elegant
A mazing Earth
R efreshing
T he Earth is amazing
H appy home.

Jamie Brown (6)
St Faith's CE Infant School, Lincoln

Earth

E arth is my home
A ll animals are different
R ocky planet
T he Earth is beautiful
H ome makes me smile.

Isobella Walker (7)
St Faith's CE Infant School, Lincoln

Earth

E arth is the only planet with life, it has lots of life
A ll of the animals either swim or swing or walk
R eally, the nicest planet to live on
T he Earth is surrounded by Venus and Mars
H ome to me.

Archie Olivier-Townrow (7)
St Faith's CE Infant School, Lincoln

Mars

M ars is the fourth planet to the sun
A red planet next to Jupiter
R ocky planet next to Earth
S o you can't go on Mars because you will die.

William Holden (6)
St Faith's CE Infant School, Lincoln

My First Acrostic 2011 - The UK

Earth

E arth is nice

A mazing it is

R ocky Earth

T he Earth is beautiful

H ome.

Isaac Atherton (7)
St Faith's CE Infant School, Lincoln

Sun

S un sizzling hot and shiny

U p in the sky

N ever to look up at the sun.

Holli-May Davison (7)
St Faith's CE Infant School, Lincoln

Earth

E legant Earth
A ll the animals are amazing
R ight next to Mars and Venus
T here are flowers
H ome.

Georgia Abbott (6)
St Faith's CE Infant School, Lincoln

Sun

S un, never been visited
U p in the sky
N ever go to the sun.

Tommy Jameson (7)
St Faith's CE Infant School, Lincoln

My First Acrostic 2011 - The UK

Earth

E arth is beautiful and it is our home

A mazing Earth

R efreshing Earth

T he Earth has life

H appy homes.

Danielle Burrows (7)
St Faith's CE Infant School, Lincoln

Jupiter

J upiter is very big

U ltra big

P lanet Jupiter is enormous

I think Jupiter is great

T errific planet

E xtremely rocky and

R eally beautiful.

Charlotte Drakard (6)
St Faith's CE Infant School, Lincoln

Jupiter

J olly good storms
U nlikely to be seen
P erfect
I t is the biggest planet
T errific planet
E xcellent planet
R eally good planet.

Oliver Wiles (6)
St Faith's CE Infant School, Lincoln

Jupiter

J olly good storms
U nlikely to be seen
P erfect planet
I like Jupiter because it has lots of lovely colours
T errific place in space
E xcellent at being a sister to Saturn
R ed spot is there because a meteor has crashed into planet Jupiter.

Anna Gill (6)
St Faith's CE Infant School, Lincoln

My First Acrostic 2011 - The UK

Super J

S uper J to the rescue
U nderground passage
P ower to defeat baddies
E lectric fire punch
R eally fast

J ust a gun.

Jonathan Rigby (6)
St Patrick's RC Primary School, Walton-le-Dale

Superheroes

S ave good people
U se special powers
P lans his rescue
E veryone's friend
R un fast
H over forever
E scapes from anywhere
R eady
O rder
E xcellent superhero
S uperheroes save the world.

Alex Bateson (6)
St Patrick's RC Primary School, Walton-le-Dale

Lily

L ily is a superstar
I like to fly in the sky
L ovely Lily
Y ou better watch out.

Lily Singleton (7)
St Patrick's RC Primary School, Walton-le-Dale

Firegirl

F abulous flames
I mpresses her friends
R oaring fire in her pocket
E legant fire
G iant fire balls
I gnores the babies
R escues people
L oves her fire.

Milly Thomas (6)
St Patrick's RC Primary School, Walton-le-Dale

My First Acrostic 2011 – The UK

Chipgirl

C an fly high
H as lots of power
I n time, perfect girl
P eaceful girl
G raceful chip girl
I ncredible girl
R eally happy flying
L eft powers.

Louana Avison (6)
St Patrick's RC Primary School, Walton-le-Dale

Superhero

S ave the day
U nderwear on a superhero
P roblem solving
E njoy fighting crime
R ight superheroes
H ates villains
E vil is bad
R ight on course
O bstacles are for superheroes who train.

Grace Brown (6)
St Patrick's RC Primary School, Walton-le-Dale

Cheetahman

C heetahman is cool
H e is a writer by day
E ats fish
E ats meat
T o the rescue
A round for 20 years
H e is calm when not hurt
M y name is Cheetahman
A lly is Snakeman
N ice when Sam Wilson.

Sam Wilson (6)
St Patrick's RC Primary School, Walton-le-Dale

Finger Girl

F inger Girl is cool
I mproved my flying lessons
N ever gives up
G oes to secret destinations
E njoyed her mission
R eady to fly to Spain

G iant villain
I was growing
R aces to everyone's rescue
L oves to laugh and smile.

Faye Houghton (7)
St Patrick's RC Primary School, Walton-le-Dale

Dream Girl

D o super things
R escues people
E ven nicer than a princess
A very nice girl
M akes you in a dream

G iggles too much
I magine you are in a dream
R eally pretty
L oves her school.

Alexandra Fliegauf (6)
St Patrick's RC Primary School, Walton-le-Dale

Sonic

S onic is fast
O il makes Sonic trip up
N ettles spike Sonic
I ce traps Sonic
C oins like Sonic.

Tidus Nixon (6)
St Patrick's RC Primary School, Walton-le-Dale

Magic Cat

M y guinea pigs are magic
A magic cat has a wand
G ives her lives to other people
I save people who are in danger
C arries a wand wherever she goes

C arries about her kittens
A lways smiling as she goes
T reats people nicely.

Erin Rigby (7)
St Patrick's RC Primary School, Walton-le-Dale

Superhero

S uper powers I have got
U ndercover always
P unch the baddies
E nd of the fight
R ule the world
H ero to save the world
E nduring the fight
R un away from the baddy
O ver the houses they go.

Matthew Simmons (7)
St Patrick's RC Primary School, Walton-le-Dale

Megamond

M agic powers
E njoy the fight
G igantic gadget
A good car
M arvellous powers
O ver the hedge he nearly got killed
N early got killed
D efeated the baddy.

Oliver Henderson (6)
St Patrick's RC Primary School, Walton-le-Dale

Superhero

S uperhero of the day
U nderstands people
P unch as hard as a baddy
E njoys getting fit
R eally fast
H ero
E njoys fighting the galaxy
R eally strong
O ver the mountains they climb.

James Danby (6)
St Patrick's RC Primary School, Walton-le-Dale

Florence

F lorence helped the soldiers
L it her lamp
O pened the hospital door
R ead books to the soldiers
E very night she carried a lamp
N ow she went around the hospital
C leaned the floors
E very day she worked hard.

Caitlin Ward (5)
St Patrick's RC Primary School, Walton-le-Dale

Snowman

S now is cold
N ow it is snowing
O ak tree is full of snow
W ater is going because it is snowing
M ice in their holes because of the snow
A nd now it is snowing
N ow it is snowing.

Taylor Howarth (6)
St Patrick's RC Primary School, Walton-le-Dale

My First Acrostic 2011 - The UK

Snowman

S now is really cold

N ow let's get our gloves

O n Saturday it snowed

W hen it snowed I played out

M y snowman melted

A nyway I will build a snowman

N ana became better when it snowed.

Olivia Grindley (5)
St Patrick's RC Primary School, Walton-le-Dale

Florence

F lorence was a nurse

L iked helping the soldiers

O pened the hospital

R eading room

E erie in the night

N ursing she loved

C arried the lamp

E very day Florence read books.

Leon Murphy (5)
St Patrick's RC Primary School, Walton-le-Dale

Winter

Winter is cold
I sit cold
Now it is winter
The snow is cold
Everything is frosty
Really cold.

Bradley Norwell (6)
St Patrick's RC Primary School, Walton-le-Dale

Samuel

Sometimes I like to play my PS3
Apples are my favourite fruit
My age is 6
Under the sea is my favourite place to be
Elephants are my favourite animals
Let's have a snowball fight.

Samuel Truscott (6)
Samuel Barlow Primary School, Clipstone

My First Acrostic 2011 – The UK

Blaize

B laize is my name
L ikes to laugh a lot
A pples I like to eat a lot
I am 7 years old
Z oos are my best place to be
E verything is a laugh to me

A boy for a brother is horrible
N anny has a friend called Macy
G ood at swimming
E llie is my best friend
L ikes to eat ice cream.

Blaize Smith (7)
Samuel Barlow Primary School, Clipstone

Macy Bradley

M y best friend is called Leah
A pples are my favourite fruit
C ricket is my favourite thing to do
Y oghurt is my favourite food

B urgers are my favourite dinner
R eece is my brother's name
A idan is my brother as well
D ad is strong
L adybirds are my favourite creatures
E ating crisps is unhealthy
Y oghurts are unhealthy.

Macy Bradley (6)
Samuel Barlow Primary School, Clipstone

Aidan Riley

A pples are my favourite fruit
I like to watch television
D addy is here
A idan is my name
N iamh is my sister

R ipe the flowers are
I am five today
L et's have a snowball fight
E llie is good
Y ou are nice.

Aidan Riley (5)
Samuel Barlow Primary School, Clipstone

School

S chool is nice
C an I go to assembly
H ot dinners are lovely
O utside is fun
O nly children allowed
L ots of toys.

Sadie Askew (5)
Sowerby CP School, Thirsk

Rats

R ats are very soft
A rat is a good pet
T hey can eat anything they want
S eeing them is hard.

Hope Smith (5)
Sowerby CP School, Thirsk

Boats On The Sea

B oats have a flag
O il makes the boats go
A nchors make the boats stop
T here are lots of boats in the harbour.

Calum Kirby (5)
Sowerby CP School, Thirsk

Climbing Cats

C limbing the gate
A nd they climb trees
T hey have sharp claws
S ometimes they go in kennels.

Francesca Kee (4)
Sowerby CP School, Thirsk

All About Me

S unny
K ind
Y oung
E xciting.

Skye Beattie (4)
Sowerby CP School, Thirsk

Castle

C ool
A mazing
S pooky
T all
L onely
E xciting.

William Kelly (4)
Sowerby CP School, Thirsk

Adam

A mazing
D ancer
A footballer
M onster.

Adam Cropper (5)
Sowerby CP School, Thirsk

Princess

P retty
R ed
I n a castle
N ice
C lever
E veryone's friend
S parkling
S hiny.

India Duree (4)
Sowerby CP School, Thirsk

My Pet

C ats jump
A cat is cuddly
T hey sleep on my bed
S ometimes they scratch.

Bethan Ballard (4)
Sowerby CP School, Thirsk

My First Acrostic 2011 - The UK

Me

R eally scary
I s a star
L ovely
E xciting
Y oung.

Riley Beighton (5)
Sowerby CP School, Thirsk

Myself

D aring
A star
N ice
I ce cool
E xciting
L ittle.

Daniel Hindmarch (5)
Sowerby CP School, Thirsk

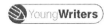

All About Me

F unny
L ovely
I s fun
S uper
S tar.

Felicity Stockdale (4)
Sowerby CP School, Thirsk

All About Me

S uper
A star
M e!

Sam Powell (4)
Sowerby CP School, Thirsk

My First Acrostic 2011 - The UK

Singing Songs

S inging songs

I s cool

N ice

G ood

I s cool

N oisy

G reat fun.

Eloise Christon (4)
Sowerby CP School, Thirsk

I Like Cats

C ats miaow

A cat can be a good pet

T ails are fluffy

S cratch with their claws.

RubyMai Cousins (5)
Sowerby CP School, Thirsk

All About Me

T all
A boy
Y oung
L ike laughing
O utside
R eally fun.

Taylor Clark (5)
Sowerby CP School, Thirsk

Computers

C ontrol
O n
M ouse
P lay
U seful
T ype
E verywhere
R eally fun
S ound.

Cameron Ord (4)
Sowerby CP School, Thirsk

Myself

K ind
Y oung
L ovely
E veryone's friend.

Kyle Pounder (5)
Sowerby CP School, Thirsk

Aaron

A nts wear nothing
A pples are round
R un on concrete
O n a scooter
N ice to my friends.

Aaron Lovell (5)
Stanwick Primary School, Wellingborough

Carla

C arries her lunch box
A te spag Bol
R ides on a train
L oves her daddy
A cts silly.

Carla Hartley (5)
Stanwick Primary School, Wellingborough

Evie

E njoys playing
V ery funny
I n the house
E ats dinner.

Evie McKay (4)
Stanwick Primary School, Wellingborough

My First Acrostic 2011 - The UK

Grace

G oes to France
R aces with my friends
A pple crumble
C ounting numbers
E gg sandwiches.

Grace Williams (5)
Stanwick Primary School, Wellingborough

Jack

J elly
A nt
C ats
K angaroo.

Jack Rhoder (4)
Stanwick Primary School, Wellingborough

Maisy-Jay

M akes cakes
A pple cake
I n the kitchen
S its on the sofa
Y ellow icing
-
J am toast
A nd butter
Y oghurt, strawberry.

Maisy-Jay Wooding (4)
Stanwick Primary School, Wellingborough

Megan

M akes cakes
E ats cakes
G ets shopping
A nd crisps
N ot oranges and pears.

Megan Stuchfield (5)
Stanwick Primary School, Wellingborough

Samuel

S illy snake
A pple pie snake
M unchy snake
U nder snake
E ggy snake
L ong snake.

Samuel Danton (4)
Stanwick Primary School, Wellingborough

Scarlett

S inging songs
C ooking cakes
A pples are good for you
R abbit ran
L oves cake
E ats apples
T astes beans
T ouch my toes.

Scarlett King (5)
Stanwick Primary School, Wellingborough

Sophie

S illy sun
O n the wall
P ink pig
H ungry horse
I cy igloo
E gg, egg, egg.

Sophie Lewis (4)
Stanwick Primary School, Wellingborough

Taylor

T ouches cakes
A nd jelly
Y ummy yoghurts
L oves my brother and
O ranges
R eads books all day.

Taylor Lewis (5)
Stanwick Primary School, Wellingborough

Yasmin

Yellow flowers

Apple

Sophie's friend

Mummy

Ice cream

Nose.

Yasmin Hussain (4)
Stanwick Primary School, Wellingborough

Darcy

Drinks orange

Apples for a snack

Runs fast

Can dance

Yellow sunshine.

Darcy Stanton (4)
Stanwick Primary School, Wellingborough

Taylor

T ouches his toys
A t home
Y ellow toys
L ikes Jonny Test
O pens presents
R eads Star Wars.

Taylor Holben (5)
Stanwick Primary School, Wellingborough

Owen

O nly eats pizza
W atches Snow White
E njoys playing with Eddie
N ice and friendly.

Owen Binks (6)
Stanwick Primary School, Wellingborough

My First Acrostic 2011 - The UK

Harley

H iccups
A lfie
R eally fun
L ikes lollipops
E ats toast
Y ippee, I like Mario.

Harley Barker (5)
Stanwick Primary School, Wellingborough

Skye

S uper CBBC
K ind and helpful
Y es I like frogs!
E ats pasta and grapes.

Skye Broomhead (6)
Stanwick Primary School, Wellingborough

Rachel

R oses
A lways happy
C heerful
H appy at school
E verything makes me happy
L ibby makes me laugh.

Rachel Hill (6)
Stanwick Primary School, Wellingborough

Haylie

H appy
A pple
Y oghurt
L ollipop
I ce cream
E ats cakes.

Haylie Smith (6)
Stanwick Primary School, Wellingborough

Eddie

E T
D angerous
D reams
I nvincible
E xpert.

Eddie Phillips (6)
Stanwick Primary School, Wellingborough

Michaela

M y friend is Rachel
I do good in my writing
C heerful
H appy
A t the beach
E xcellent
L ovely
A lways helpful.

Michaela Dunn (6)
Stanwick Primary School, Wellingborough

Lola

L ikes my rabbit
O ranges are juicy
L ikes going to the park
A rgues with Mummy.

Lola Vukovic (5)
Stanwick Primary School, Wellingborough

Caleb

C aleb is fun
A lways happy
L ola is my friend
E ats pizza
B all.

Caleb Neithercut (5)
Stanwick Primary School, Wellingborough

Bethan

- **B** right
- **E** ats spaghetti
- **T** eddy bear is fluffy
- **H** appy when playing
- **A** lways quiet
- **N** ormally wears glasses.

Bethan Fraser (5)
Stanwick Primary School, Wellingborough

Harris

- **H** elpful
- **A** lways friendly
- **R** eally happy
- **R** acing my brother
- **I** ce skating is fun
- **S** onic the Hedgehog.

Harris John (5)
Stanwick Primary School, Wellingborough

Madeline

M aking cakes

A lways playing drawing

D ad

E mily

L ike to eat pancakes

I watch Thomas the Tank Engine

N ice and kind

E verything pink.

Madeline Williams (5)
Stanwick Primary School, Wellingborough

Tamzin

T rying my best

A s cute as a rose

M cDonald's is my favourite

Z ebras are my favourite animals

I like to play on my Wii

N ice as can be.

Tamzin Lineham (7)
Stanwick Primary School, Wellingborough

Harrison

- H ome
- A wesome
- R un
- R un very fast
- I watch football
- S uper
- O llie is my friend
- N aughty.

Harrison Shouler (6)
Stanwick Primary School, Wellingborough

Heidi

- H orse riding is fun
- E ggs are yummy
- I njections hurt me
- D onkeys make me laugh
- I ce cream cools me down.

Heidi Long (6)
Stanwick Primary School, Wellingborough

Charlie

C ool as an apple
H appy as a rose
A very nice person
R uns as fast as Alfie
L ikes to play on the Wii
I like ice cream
E ats lots of ice cream.

Charlie Russell (7)
Stanwick Primary School, Wellingborough

Ryan

R unning champion
Y oghurt is yummy
A mazing work
N ice.

Ryan Smith (7)
Stanwick Primary School, Wellingborough

My First Acrostic 2011 - The UK

Megan Breakwell

M cDonald's make her happy

E ggs make her ache

G oes quackers every day

A fter school it's time to play on the Wii

N ever naughty.

Megan Breakwell (7)
Stanwick Primary School, Wellingborough

Ciaran

C ool as a cat

I like gerbils

A nimal lover

R uns fast

A big scoffer

N utty.

Ciaran Baggott (7)
Stanwick Primary School, Wellingborough

Callum

C ute as a hamster

A lways popular

L oveable

L ovely as a pig

U nusual person

M ore excited than anyone.

Callum Castle-Palmer (6)
Stanwick Primary School, Wellingborough

Craig

C limbing very well

R un very well

A ll my friends like me

I am like a monkey

G ood as a dinosaur.

Craig Dodson (7)
Stanwick Primary School, Wellingborough

William

W icked
I like my dad
L iking people
L etting people play
I like my sister
A pples are my favourite
M ummy takes me to school.

William Hobbs (6)
Stanwick Primary School, Wellingborough

Toby

T ogether is strong
O n all day
B agged with excitement
Y ummy as can be.

Toby Johnson (7)
Stanwick Primary School, Wellingborough

Morgan

M ad
O range
R eading is good
G ames are cool
A nd my dad makes me happy
N ice.

Morgan Lewis (7)
Warwick Primary School, Wellingborough

Luke

L ikes computers
U mbrella ride is my favourite
K ind
E njoys playing.

Luke Hughes (7)
Warwick Primary School, Wellingborough

Bobby

B lue is my favourite colour
O bsessed with the puppy
B aking cakes is fun
B uilding with my Lego
Y ou are my best friend.

Bobby Ireland (6)
Warwick Primary School, Wellingborough

Robin

R oll
O ranges
B eautiful
I play with the ice
N ice.

Robin Bayes (7)
Warwick Primary School, Wellingborough

Henry

H elpful
E at healthy food
N ice to my friends
R ushing around
Y oung.

Henry Lawley (7)
Warwick Primary School, Wellingborough

Kian

K ind
I like sleeping out
A pples are my favourite
N ice.

Kian Brown (6)
Warwick Primary School, Wellingborough

Jack

J okes with everyone
A lways plays with cars
C aring
K ind.

Jack Presley (6)
Warwick Primary School, Wellingborough

Chanelle

C aring
H appy
A licia is my sister
N ice
E njoys playing with Jack
L augh
L ike my hamster
E xcellent at writing.

Chanelle McFarlane (6)
Warwick Primary School, Wellingborough

Rico

R ock I climb
I like playing tag
C ool
O range I like.

Rico Fensom (6)
Warwick Primary School, Wellingborough

Taylor

T idying my room
A lways drawing pictures
Y oung
L oving
O n the phone
R unning round.

Taylor Savage (6)
Warwick Primary School, Wellingborough

My First Acrostic 2011 - The UK

Corey

C aterpillar
O ctopus
R ain
E lephant
Y o-yo.

Corey Tyler (6)
Warwick Primary School, Wellingborough

Amber

A mber loves apples
M y favourite colour is pink
B ambi is my nickname
E ating chocolate is what I like
R eading is my hobby to do.

Amber Davis (6)
Warwick Primary School, Wellingborough

Ellie

E njoys playing
L ove swimming
L ove friends
I like ice cream
E njoys going to the park.

Ellie Knighton (6)
Warwick Primary School, Wellingborough

Raajus

R egularly I play with computer
A ll the time I read in library
A lye is my sister's name
J uice is my favourite drink
U s, family is important to me
S andman was bad in a movie.

Raajus Dewan (7)
Warwick Primary School, Wellingborough

My First Acrostic 2011 - The UK

Rebekah

R ebekah likes her teacher lots
E ats healthy food
B e good in class
E xcited about being a big sister
K ind
A ge is seven
H er favourite animal is a husky dog.

Rebekah Shaw (7)
Warwick Primary School, Wellingborough

Logan

L ikes yellow fish
O ften plays games
G oes to Beavers
A lways happy with my dad
N ice.

Logan Westrop (6)
Warwick Primary School, Wellingborough

Kia

K ind to my friends
I s very helpful
A s pretty as a picture.

Kia Abbott (7)
Warwick Primary School, Wellingborough

All About Shaun

S nake is my favourite
H appy
A lways good
U nderstands science
N ice.

Shaun Rupere
Warwick Primary School, Wellingborough

All About Lucy

L ovely and little
U se my hands to draw
C urls in my hair
Y ellow is my favourite.

Lucy Gregory
Warwick Primary School, Wellingborough

Sky

S parkly glitter hairband
K ittens are my favourite
Y ellow is my favourite colour.

Sky Sharp (7)
Warwick Primary School, Wellingborough

All About Me

L ovely and little
O ranges are my favourite fruit
U nder the sea is where I like to hide
I love chocolate
S eashells are my favourite things
E ating my breakfast, yum-yum.

Louise Sharp
Warwick Primary School, Wellingborough

Ella

E lla loves to play
L oves to laugh
L oves to eat apples
A nnoys everyone.

Ella Louise Skeen (6)
Warwick Primary School, Wellingborough

My First Acrostic 2011 - The UK

Me

E njoys playing with friends
L istens well
L oves chocolate
I nterested in dogs
E xcited.

Ellie Jones-King
Warwick Primary School, Wellingborough

Me

T iny
I love playing with Stella
A lways smiling.

Tia Warwick-Compton
Warwick Primary School, Wellingborough

Super Sava

S uper
A dventurous
V ery fast
A lways playing football.

Sava Trkulja
Warwick Primary School, Wellingborough

Chloe The Great

C uddly
H ide-and-seek is my favourite
L ovely
O n the playground I play tig
E at all my lunch.

Chloe Bates
Warwick Primary School, Wellingborough

All About Charlie

C hocolate

H appy

A rtist

R uns fast

L ikes sweets and

I ce cream

E xciting.

Charlie Rogers (6)
Warwick Primary School, Wellingborough

Super Cameron

C aring

A mazing

M ice are my favourite

E njoy school

R ooney is the best

O ranges are my favourite

N ever shows off.

Cameron Daniels (7)
Warwick Primary School, Wellingborough

Really Cool Ramzan

R acing
A lways fast
M oney collector
Z ooming
A ngel
N ever naughty.

Ramzan Ali
Warwick Primary School, Wellingborough

Sean

S ean is playing a soldier
E veryday he plays with his sister
A practise of tap and ballet
N ever gets cross.

Sean Appleton (6)
Welbourn CE Primary School, Lincoln

My First Acrostic 2011 - The UK

Darci Rose

D arci is delightful
A lways kind
R eally cheeky
C hloe is my friend
I love horses

R osie cheeks
O ne of the best in the class
S ilent on the carpet
E veryone is my friend.

Darci Rose John (6)
Welbourn CE Primary School, Lincoln

Rachael

R achael has blue eyes
A nnie is her best friend
C heerful
H olly is her cousin
A nd is good at adding up
E xtremely kind
L ikes the environment.

Rachael Bain (6)
Welbourn CE Primary School, Lincoln

Patrick

P lays with the DS
A lways happy
T ries very hard
R eads books
I sabella is his friend
C heerful
K ind to his friends.

Patrick Mack (5)
Welbourn CE Primary School, Lincoln

Jack

J elly is my favourite food
A good footballer
C learly good at kicking a ball
K ing of the goal.

Jack Livingstone (7)
Welbourn CE Primary School, Lincoln

My First Acrostic 2011 – The UK

Molly Grace

M y friends are Jasmine, Izzy and Rosie
O n the weekend I like to play with my Sylvanians
L ike my sister called Mary and my brother called Sam
L ove my mum and dad
Y ou can see me in class 1

G reat at driving the jeep
R eally funny
A t the stables I have friends
C an do horse jumping
E xtremely polite.

Molly Holmes (7)
Welbourn CE Primary School, Lincoln

Lewis

L ewis likes playing on the Wii
E veryday he is a chatterbox
W illiam is his friend
I s good at making pizza
S ays boo!

Lewis Stewart (5)
Welbourn CE Primary School, Lincoln

Tom

T om loves playing the piano
O n the Wii he always wins
M ost of the time he likes Saturdays.

Tom Livingstone (5)
Welbourn CE Primary School, Lincoln

Chloe

C aring
H appy
L ovely
O n the weekends she plays
E veryone likes Chloe.

Chloe Francis (4)
Welbourn CE Primary School, Lincoln

Isabella

I zzy is my name
S ings songs
A lways happy
B irthday on Friday
E njoys dancing
L oves pink
L ikes Barbie dolls
A nother year older.

Isabella Morris (4)
Welbourn CE Primary School, Lincoln

Teddy

T hinker
E ddie is my friend
D addy works for Lives
D IY I enjoy
Y esterday I had sweets.

Teddy Tottingham (5)
Welbourn CE Primary School, Lincoln

Young Writers Information

We hope you have enjoyed reading this book - and that you will continue to enjoy it in the coming years.

If you like reading and writing poetry drop us a line, or give us a call, and we'll send you a free information pack.

Alternatively if you would like to order further copies of this book or any of our other titles, then please give us a call or log onto our website at www.youngwriters.co.uk.

Young Writers Information
Remus House
Coltsfoot Drive
Peterborough
PE2 9BF
(01733) 890066